42

by Rusty Busby

D1437960

DORRANCE
PUBLISHING CO
EST. 1920
PITTSBURGH, PENNSYLVANIA 15238

Dorrance Publishing Co
585 Alpha Drive
Pittsburgh, PA 15238
Visit our website at *www.dorrancebookstore.com*

ISBN: 979-8-88812-294-5
eISBN: 979-8-88812-794-0

My friend, Judi Youngers, whom I consider to be the "Poet Laureate of Comfort" has written a marvelous poem about our 42 game in the domino parlor. She has graciously allowed me to include it herein.

The Domino Parlor

Drag out the worn enameled tables, two
should do fine, the ones branding a frosty brew.
Grab 'hold those rusty folding chairs, slumped
against the feedbags, see them there in the dim of the
corrugated rust and planked wood floor. Now watch
the altogether too-damned much traffic as you haul
your load across High Street. Just plunk it down
on the sidewalk in front of the ruined general store.

Game's on . . . 42 that is.
Posted signs gone, though, "Domino Parlor,"
"Law West of the Guadalupe" victims of so-called
upscaling and all that. A "Reserved Event Setting"
replaces the vernacular. Pick-ups parked,
the domino players drift in, a little paunchier,
hair thinning or disappeared. Absent, too,
reserve mode, Sunday manners.

Of course, there's no order, no protocol.
With a gallery of two or more friends, wives, drop-ins,
and the just plain curious settling on the limestone steps,
the visitin', town gossip, and ribbing revs up.
It's a ritual, you see. Friday, late afternoon,
bring your cooler. Dried venison sausage might be good
to snack on, deviled eggs, whatever trips your trigger.
No foo-foo food, though.

Rain, sleet snow, a below-zero gauge,
more often than not, the game's still a "go"
perhaps moved up the block to the back room
of Jim's, once Gael's Barber Shop. While you are at it,
scan the other side of the street near the café tables
where the millennials now gather, costumed
in strappy heels and fancy boots, dressed
way too skimpy for November's cool down.

Tourists wonder at the spectacle, chalk it up
to small-town "quaint and curious," jump
at sudden guffaws echoing 'cross the crowded street.
Held game tiles tap impatience, signal a next play,
then clack down hard on tabletop. My hands-down choice
the game goes on: no law, no order, even though
I don't play. Yes, I've become an old-timer; for certain,
irregular, choosing local color and customs to stay.

Judi Youngers, 2022

Contents

Prologue

Domino, noun / dom-i-no / da-me-no. If, when you hear the word, your first thought is slang for "giving birth", then this book is probably not for you. But, if in your mind you can conjure up the sound of someone "shakin' them bones", and the sound gives you that little prickly sensation between your shoulder blades, and at the base of your neck, then read on. You've come to the right place.

Domino, in France a long hooded black cape worn to a masquerade ball

Chapter One

General History of Dominos

Domino actually has two meanings. One, it was a long-hooded cloak worn with a half-mask as a costume to a masquerade ball or during carnival season. The second, a flat rectangular block (of bone, ivory, wood, or plastic) whose face is divided into two equal parts that are blank or bear usually from one to six dots arranged as on dice faces. Each domino is twice as long as it is wide.

The earliest mention of dominos comes from the 13th century in China. Italian missionaries to China are credited with bringing dominos back to Italy in the early 18th century. Dominos then moved on to France and England after 1750.

In France, dominos were once made of ebony with ivory faces, which brought to mind the black cape worn by a priest under his white surplice. Not to suggest that dominos, especially 42, is a divine experience.

While 42 may not be divine, it is most definitely a spiritual event. This is borne out in *The Hitchhiker's Guide to the Galaxy* by Douglas Adams, which is a science fiction comedy about an Englishman named Arthur Dent. After the earth was destroyed, Arthur learns, through his travels, that the earth was a giant supercomputer created by another supercomputer named Deep Thought. The purpose of Deep Thought was to provide the answer to the

"Ultimate Question of Life, The Universe and Everything". After eons of calculations that answer was given as "42".

We all remember our childhood domino games with Mom or Dad or Grandma or Grandpa. We played "regular" or "straight" dominos. The only thing you had to do initially was add up to 5 or 10 or a multiple thereof. This was the first math lesson for many of us. It even helped me pass math and graduate to the second grade. We learned terms like "spinner", "boneyard", "dominoed", and "blocked". Whoever dominoed first got all the points, to the nearest five, that were in their opponent's hand. The first player to reach 250 points won the game.

Chapter Two

Texas Style, The Birth of 42

In 1887 in Trappe Spring, Texas (now Garner) west of Ft. Worth, two young boys, William Thomas and Walter Earl, loved to play cards. Playing cards, however, was considered to be the work of the devil according to their Baptist teachings of that day and time. Unfortunately (or fortunately for the rest of Texas) they got caught by their parents. They both got a whipping, but the boys' love of cards made them seek an alternative. Since dominos were not sinful, they invented a card game with dominos, and that game was 42. The game spread far and wide throughout Texas until it became known as the "National Game of Texas".

This book is not intended to teach you how to play 42, nor is it a recitation of the rules, especially since we don't always follow the rules, and we occasionally make up some new ones. Widely considered to be the Bible of 42 is Dennis Roberson's *Winning 42, Strategy & Lore of the National Game of Texas*, 5th Edition, Updated and Expanded, Texas Tech University Press. Roberson's book not only teaches you how to play 42, but it turns novices into veterans and veterans into even better players. It explains the rules and guidelines, as do other resources, but it is the only book that delves into the strategy of 42. If you really want to learn to play 42, buy Roberson's book and hook up with a 42 game and observe how the game is played.

I still feel compelled to give you a few basics about how the game is played. The first four players at the domino parlor will each draw a domino. The players with the two highest dominos will be partners against the two players with the lowest dominos. Someone will shake the dominos and each player will draw one domino. The player drawing the highest domino will begin by giving the other players a shake. Each player will draw seven dominos with the shaker drawing last. The player to the left of the shaker will bid first or pass. The bidding goes around the table until all four players have had an opportunity to bid. The highest bidder will get to name the trump. If the first three players all pass, then the fourth (the "shaker") is forced to take the bid for at least the minimum 30 bid.

Trump, named after "triumph", is the suit that the winning bidder believes will help him win the hand. Trumps can be a particular suit, blanks through sixes. Another bid is "doubles are trumps" or "doubles are a suit of their own". Another option is to bid "no trump" or "follow me".

Bidding is based on the number of points that you think you can make in a hand. There are 42 points that can be made in each hand: five points for each 5-pointer (5/0, 4/1, 3/2); ten points for each 10-pointer (5/5, 6/4); and one point for each trick taken (7 points). The minimum bid is 30. Once the bid reaches 42 or 1 mark, you can only overbid by 1-mark increments. An exception to this is that the opening bidder may bid 2 marks or 84.

There are some variations to the regular bidding process. A bidder may "splash" which means that the bidder has 3 doubles. If he is successful in obtaining the bid, his partner must name the trump and begins play. If the bid is successful, you earn 3 marks; if it is not, your opponent earns 3 marks. A bidder can also "plunge", which means that the bidder has 4 doubles, and the hand is played the same as a splash except a plunge is worth 4 marks. A first bidder may also bid 1 or 2 marks "nello" or "low". This means that he believes that he will not take any tricks.

Once all the bidding has been completed, we're ready to play 42. Whenever a domino is led, the following players must follow suit if they are able. If they cannot follow suit, they can play any domino they choose, including a trump. If they do not follow suit and they could have, then they renege, and when they are caught that team loses the point. Whoever wins the trick gets to lead on the next trick. One of the most difficult things for new players to remember is that the large end of the domino controls unless the small end is a trump, and in that case the trump controls. For example, if you lead the 6/3, then it is a 6 and all the other players must play a 6, unless 3 is the trump and then it is a 3. Also, you need to remember that "a domino laid is a domino played". Once you play a domino, you cannot take it back.

Play continues until all seven tricks have been played or a winner is determined before the last trick is played. For example, if the bid is 31 and the bidding team already has 34 points after four tricks, then you will usually declare the bidder as a winner for that hand and there is no need to play it out. It becomes a "lay down". All players will turn their remaining dominos face up to make sure that no one reneged. If the bid is one or more marks high then the dominos are double stacked after each trick, and players are not allowed to pick up the stacked dominos. In all one or more-mark bids, the bidder and his partner must take all seven tricks. Should they even lose one trick they would be set and would lose that hand. If the bid is one or more marks low or nello, the dominos are not stacked, and the bidder's partner turns his dominos facedown and does not play. The bidder must lead and may not take any tricks. If he loses even one trick, he is set.

Scoring is accomplished in one of two ways: the first team to reach 250 points; or the first team to receive seven marks. I have never played a 42 game in my 70 years of playing where we kept a numerical score. If you want to play to 250 you will have to look it up. Marks are kept by one of the players who is the scorekeeper. Marks are recorded in several different ways: 1111111; 11111-11, ALL, or SEX. I think I learned that last one in college. I've been playing 42 since I was about 5. My mom and dad loved to play with friends and family, and they taught me how to play.

I remember going to Seguin to visit my mom's mother, Ma-Maw, and Ma-Maw's sister and her family. They would immediately break out the beer and get a 42 game going out on the front porch. The players were my Ma-Maw, my great aunt, Ella, and her husband, Bucket, as well as my mom and dad, and Mom's cousins: Kenneth Ray, Arthur Lee and her brother, Fritz. I ain't making these names up, y'all. I didn't know Bucket had another name until I was grown. It turned out to be Adolph.

I loved watching them play and slapping the dominos down on the table. My cousins and I would not get to play until after the game was over, but we could watch. You do learn a lot about 42 just by watching and paying attention. They spoke German a lot of the time, so I also learned a foreign language. However, most of the words that I retained were curse words.

I also learned how to cheat. If you laid out the 3/2 domino with the 3-end pointed toward your partner, that was a signal to your partner that you had the double 3. So, if he had a 3 off, he could lead that, and you would be able to catch the trick for your team. If you did not have a 3 to lead, but you had the 2/1, you could spin the domino to the right when you threw it out on the table. That would tell your partner to add the 2 and 1 together to show him that you had the double 3. On the other hand, if you had the 6/3 and you spun it to the left, your partner would know to subtract the two numbers to tell him that you had the double 3. Not that my saintly Ma-Maw or I ever cheated.

I continued to play through high school with family and friends. When I went to the University of Texas, I played a lot. After class, we would race back to the Delta Upsilon fraternity house at noon to make sure we got a seat at the 42 table to play and watch the new TV sensation, "Batman".

After law school when I started my law practice, my 42 games were not as frequent. I remember when I was practicing in Amarillo, and I was defending a man accused of felony theft in Canyon. We were trying the case in the old Randall County Courthouse. We had concluded the evidence and the jury was deliberating.

They had been out several hours, when the bailiff, Gene, came to me and said he thought the jury was playing 42 in the jury room. We listened at the door and sure enough you could hear them shaking those bones and slapping them down on the table. The bailiff said that they kept the dominos in the drawer of the conference table in the jury room because courthouse employees would go in there during lunch and play 42. I told him he needed to go tell the judge.

The judge immediately had the bailiff bring the jury back in the courtroom and after verifying that they were playing dominos he severely chastised them, took their dominos away and sent them back in the jury room to deliberate. I moved for a mistrial because of the unusual circumstances, but the judge denied my motion and sent them back to continue deliberations. After a short time, the jury sent out a note saying they were hopelessly deadlocked and could not reach a unanimous verdict. The judge granted my motion for a mistrial, and he released the jury. I was talking to one of the jurors afterwards and he said that they were hung up on reaching a verdict and got bored and found the dominos in the drawer, so they started playing 42. It turned out that there were only three jurors who wanted to find my client guilty, so the State decided not to re-try my client and they dismissed the case. I guess you could say that 42 saved my client's bacon.

42 is such a great game. The best way to learn the game is to just start playing it with some people that already know how. You will pick it up in no time.

Rusty's office and house on 7th Street in Comfort

Rainbow Bread Bench, Rusty, John McCurdy,
Bobbye Burow, Clarence, and Eddie

Chapter Three

42 in Comfort (Texas, That Is)

In 1995, I grew tired of life in the big city of Austin. Too many people, too much traffic and too many lawyers. I decided to end my fourth tour living in Austin. My folks lived on a little spread, La Hipoteca Ranch, outside of Boerne. I decided that I needed to just become a country lawyer and move back "home". I started looking around Boerne and there was already 30+ lawyers actively practicing law. It was beginning to look a lot like Austin.

One afternoon I drove up to Comfort to look around and found that there was only one other lawyer in town. I fell in love with the quaint little town of Comfort. So, I bought two little houses which were side by side. I lived in one and hung out my shingle in the other . I became friends with Gregory Krauter, one of the owners of the Ingenhuett General Store which at that time was the oldest continuously operating general store in Texas. Tragically the store burned down on March 18, 2006. After getting Greg's permission, I ran an ad in the Comfort News announcing that we would begin gathering on the sidewalk in front of Ingenhuett's on Fridays to play 42, drink beer and whiskey and discuss all the pertinent issues in the world. The response was overwhelming. We've been there almost every Friday since October 1995.

Our little "domino parlor" was off and running. There was an old Rainbow Bread bench on the sidewalk next to the outside wall of Ingenhuett's. We would set up a table, so that one player could sit on the bench and then the other three would sit in chairs around the table. The "Salt House" is across High Street from the domino parlor. It had been used by Ingenhuett's to store salt but is currently used for storage. Greg gave us permission to store our tables, chairs, and other domino paraphernalia there. This keeps us from having to transport all our "equipment" every week. We've been through a whole lot of tables, the latest being a metal and enamel topped "Corona" table. It has proven to be the best, as it is fairly light, and each leg has two containers welded to them to hold your beer or other drinks. It also makes a great sound when you slap them bones down.

I had a huge rock at my law office in Comfort with the following inscription: "Law West of the Guadalupe". This wording was of course borrowed (or stolen) from the Hon. Roy Bean; and the Guadalupe River runs through Comfort. Since Comfort does not have any local government, we decided that the "Law West of the Guadalupe" would be the governing authority over the domino parlor. With that in mind we put up a street sign prohibiting parking in the domino parlor on Fridays. It reads "No Parking in the Domino Parlor, Every Friday from 3:30 p.m. to 12 Midnight. By the Order of Law West of the Guadalupe".

It did not take long for "the" 42 domino game in Comfort to take on a life of its own. The game has evolved and continues to evolve over the years. It's sort of like Willie Nelson's answer as to why he likes Texas so much—cuz nobody's in charge. Nobody is truly in charge of the domino game either. It's just a bunch of ne'er do wells doing what we do so well.

We have played at several different locations due to weather or other circumstances. Gael's Barber Shop is just down the street and is run by Jim Moore. Gael Montana was a player before she passed away and Jim still plays. Jim just gave several of us skeleton keys that open the front door of the "Barber Ship" and gave us permission to play there even if he was gone. We have also played under the covered deck of High's Café which is across the street from the domino parlor. Wesley Atkison has had us over to the Cabana Hut at his pool, and we've gone to Jack and Rhonda Hall's up in Center Point, because Rhonda always feeds really good.

Salt House on High Street

Rusty's Law Office in Comfort, Gregory Krauter, Rusty

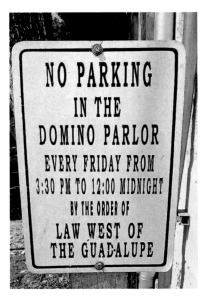

No Parking Sign on High Street in Comfort

Gael's Barber Ship on High Street

In past years when we were younger, we would gut it out like the postal carriers; "neither rain, nor snow, nor sleet, nor hail shall keep us from our appointed rounds." When it was real cold Wesley would bring a propane heater and fire it up, or we would get the old, galvanized trash can out and fill it with wood and light 'er up. It could also get pretty hot in the summertime. To get a little relief we would get the window unit out and put it on top of the trash can and plug it in.

There are several things about the mechanics of a domino game in Comfort that need to be pointed out. After the game begins, the "shake" rotates to the left after the completion of a hand. That seems pretty simple, and it is, except after the beer and whiskey start to have some effect, it becomes difficult to remember whose turn it is to shake the bones. Eddie Vogt came up with a novel idea. He would wear a gimme cap and he would turn the bill of the cap toward the person who would be shaking next.

That did not work for long because Eddie would forget to move his cap. We started placing an object on the table to the left of the person who was shaking. At the conclusion of that hand the next "shaker" would be responsible for moving the item to his left. See how confusing this gets right away, but it's still the best way that we have found. We have been through several "markers". The first was a chicken. It was one of those that would lay an egg when you squeeze it. We used several others but have pretty much stuck with a small skunk.

It is very interesting to also watch how players pick up their dominos after the shake. My Ma-Maw would pick up four with one hand and three with her other hand and look at them. That always amazed me, and she did it every time without fail. I pick mine up and line them up in a straight vertical line. No one else lines them up that way. Most will make two rows with four in the front row and three in the back row. If you are observant, you can tell a lot about your opponent's hand by the way he lines up his dominos. If he gets the bid, he will usually line up all his trumps in one row. As play begins you can tell how many trumps he has. The same applies if his partner gets the bid. Sometimes a player will line up all his count in a row, or in a group.

Another thing that always happens is when somebody drops a domino on the ground if it lands face up everybody looks to see what it is, and some player yells what the domino is.

Keeping score is an interesting aspect of the game. I am the official score-keeper, simply because I am better at it, at least I claim to be. I am constantly accused of "pencil whipping" the other team, when in reality, I pencil whip my team about as often as vise-versa. Most people write Us and Them; I use We and Thee. It sounds more Biblical. We keep score on the front and back of every page in a spiral notebook. On the front of each notebook, we write the starting date and the ending date. I probably have every notebook we have ever used. There are some funny notes in the notebooks—one day I will go back and read them all. The only absolute requirement is that Wesley is forbidden from ever keeping score—he skips pages and therefore wastes space in the notebook.

There are some things that were just repeated so often that they have become part of the ritual. Every time Eddie gets set going low, he says: "I had it after that." Now everyone says it for him even if it is not true. Every time a player reneges and tries to get the domino back after he's already played, he immediately says "honest mistake". That works sometimes and not others. We had one player who was not in tune with the game at all. He never could get it that the big end of the domino controlled—the 5/2 was a 5 and not a 2, unless 2's were trumps. Every time a domino was played that had a 2 on it, he would say "Is that a duck?" We ran him off, but to this day anytime a player leads a 2/1 or a 2/0, some player will pop off with, "Is that a duck?" Alton Briggs was a good player and when he made an exceptional play and had made his mark he would always say, "Brilliant."

My dad, Bille Busby, was a long-time player. He started teaching me when I was about five. He lived to be 97. What a great ride he had. During his last years he didn't come to the domino parlor as much. He said we played too wild and crazy.

Clarence Burow was one of the original members of our merry band. He loved 42 as much as, or more than, most of the other players. Unfortunately, Clarence passed away several years ago. His wife, Bobbye, is a regular almost every Friday. She does not play, but she loves to be present and visit with all there. As you can imagine, we are all very vocal and after a hand has been completed there will be some spirited conversation, otherwise known as a loud argument over who played what, how it should have been played, how your partner lost the hand, or some other equally mundane subject about the

Score Keeping Notebook

Clarence is surprised he got the bid, Wesley, Jan and Kathleen Hughes

hand. Bobbye will let it go on for a bit until she gets tired of the arguing and then she shouts: "That was the last hand, get over it."

There is a historical marker on a limestone monument on the sidewalk at Ingenhuett's honoring the German Freethinkers, who settled in Comfort beginning in 1854. This marker contains the wording first approved by the Texas Historical Commission concerning the Freethinkers. After complaints from a few locals, THC went through several revisions which eliminated some accurate historical facts. Their final revision is on a post in the Comfort Park.

Not being pleased with the inaccuracies, Greg took the wording from the original historically accurate marker and had his own bronze marker cast and attached it to the monument. We, of course, placed a few dominos inside the monument prior to it being closed. This episode, which played out over a couple of years, is the subject of my next book in the small-town Texas series, "The Rock".

Bill Smith, whose real name was Jan Smith, loved to watch the game. He has since passed away. He had severe narcolepsy and he would usually sit on the end of the Rainbow Bread bench. Pretty soon he would be laying over on the player next to him sound asleep. One day I got a call from Kathleen Hughes, who lived a couple of blocks down from the parlor. She said a car came racing through her yard and crashed into some yard furniture. She called the sheriff's office to report the incident. She went to check on the driver and it was ol' Bill, and he was still asleep, but was not injured. I jumped in my truck and went down to the scene of the crime. Bill was starting to wake up and Kathleen did not want to get him in any trouble. The deputy sheriff wasn't there yet, so I suggested that we all haul it. I had somebody drive Bill's car and Bill home, I left in my truck, and even though it was Kathleen's house she took off too. All is well that ends well.

A few years ago, I found a hand carved monkey about eight inches tall. He is raising his right arm and hand giving the "middle finger salute". The finger was accidentally broken off, so I replaced it with part of a pipe cleaner. I put a golden chain around his neck and named him Wesley. He continues to oversee our games.

We periodically change the rules, make up new rules, and even make up new games. We always vote on it though just to make it legal. I must apologize

The Founding Freethinkers Monument on High Street

Wesley, the hand carved monkey

to Dennis Roberson again. We do not play "pure" 42 and we don't follow all the tournament rules. We play our own brand of 42. But you should learn it the right way first, so begin by reading Mr. Roberson's book.

One of the first alterations came when we decided that if it was late in the day, players could trade dominos. After all players have selected their seven dominos, a player is allowed to trade a domino with either or both of his opponents. If someone wants to trade, they select the domino they are trading, place it on the table face down and consummate the trade. You may make as many trades as you like as long as some other player will trade with you, but you may not trade with your own partner.

We had to make another rule about cell phones—no cell phones in the domino parlor. There is nothing more disruptive than a player getting a call on his cell phone during the game. If that player chooses to violate the rule and answer the call, the other players start yelling and making it impossible to hear, including saying ugly things to or about the caller.

There is a game called "Sevens". It is a variation of regular 42. Eddie always wants to play it, but it is worse than having to play moon. Just to keep Eddie from whining about it, we let him play it only on his birthday, which greatly reduces the number of times we have to suffer through it.

We went through a period of time (before High Street got so crowded) where, after the 42 game ended, we would all get in our vehicles and drive all the way down to 7th Street, backwards.

Occasionally a game will be played where one side makes no marks at all. They lose the game 7 to 0. The 0's have officially been "skunked". We bought some little furry skunks and tied leather straps around their necks. If your team gets skunked, then you and your partner must wear the skunk around your neck until there is another team that gets skunked. Clarence brought a new player into the group and immediately we all told Clarence what we thought of his new man. As it turned out he didn't like him very much either. We were having a hard time getting rid of him. One day we skunked him and his partner. He refused to wear the skunk. We told him that he could no longer play if he could not follow the rules. He never showed up after that. If we had known it would have been that easy, we would have done it sooner.

If you make no marks in a game you get skunked

We eventually found ourselves playing games that seemed to last forever, so over a few Friday sessions we created "Skunk Dominos". This is a fast version of regular 42. The minimum bid is 32 and if you have 3 doubles or 4 doubles you are "strongly advised" to splash or plunge. In this game you can win (or lose) a game in 2 or 3 hands. The other variation is that if all four players pass then you re-shake the dominos and bid again. If you re-shake three times and there is still no bid, then all players pass one domino to the left and then bid. You continue in that manner until some player bids.

None of the folks in our merry little band are bashful. They will tell you straight up that you are not worth a damn as a 42 player, and you should go find a tiddlywinks group to join. If you want to play with us, you need to develop a thick skin if you don't already have one.

Some folks say we are not serious 42 players. That may be truthful, but we are very serious about "our" game of 42, otherwise we would not continue playing as we have for the last 27 years.

Chapter Four

Memories of 27 Years of 42

As you can imagine, after 27 years there are many, many stories that are worth repeating. I am including some of my favorites.

FOOD. Every activity (inside or out) always involves food. We always have cakes or cookies to celebrate the birthdays of all our cast. We have set up a grill to cook hamburgers and hot dogs on occasion. Chili always comes to mind, and we have on numerous occasions set up a tripod with a fire underneath it to cook a great pot of chili. Every month or so, the "tamale man" comes by and sells us a few dozen homemade tamales (bean, pork, or jalapeno) which are mostly consumed on site. He represents a church group in San Antonio that is selling the tamales as a fundraiser.

We also regularly have salty snacks and deer sausage, either homemade or store-bought. Whenever a link of hard sausage shows up someone will pull a pocket knife out of their jeans to slice the sausage. The first comment will invariably be "You didn't use that knife to clean the dog poop off your boots, did you?" It does not matter what the answer is as the knife will be used anyway.

We are fortunate to also be across the street from High's Café. Denise Rabalais would occasionally bring us sweets that had outlived their salability, knowing that old pirates such as ourselves would gladly welcome them. Deborah

Atkison has a shop, Alley on High, down the street from the parlor and she often brings us chocolates that are to die for. It is safe to say that nobody goes hungry in the parlor.

PARVIN HOFFMAN: Parvin was a real character. He was already in his nineties when he showed up one day and fell right in with everyone. He had recently returned after having completed a trip through the south where he bought old wagons of all kinds and had them shipped back to Boerne. He would fix them up and sell them. His health was failing, and his family put him in a nursing home in Boerne. Well, that just wouldn't do. Often someone would go by the nursing home and check him out and bring him to the parlor to shake some bones. He loved it.

One day I noticed that he had a thin leather strap around his neck with a little leather bag on it. I asked what that was, and he opened the bag and pulled out a small bottle of Tabasco. I asked why he carried that around with him and he explained that the food at the nursing home was worse than bad. He made it a little better by putting Tabasco on it. Somebody continuously stole his bottle of Tabasco, which led him to carry it around with him.

His family finally put a stop to us checking him out of the nursing home as every time we brought him back, he had somehow been able to drink quite a bit of beer. He began to escape from the nursing home by walking off. They usually found him down at the convenience store buying beer or food.

His family eventually moved him down to a nursing home at the coast. Miss Jan and I went by to see him one time and he was still carrying his Tabasco around with him.

I'm sure he's passed on and is in heaven preparing the domino parlor in the sky for the rest of us. Eddie showed up one day and said ol' Parvin passed, and he showed us a photo of Parvin's headstone that said "Parvin Hoffmann, Never Bid With a Five Off, *****42*****". Eddie finally admitted that he photoshopped the headstone and the photo was not real. But I'm pretty sure ol' Parvin would approve.

Parvin Hoffman's [fake] headstone

SHOTGUN WEDDING: I think you can safely say that we have done just about everything at the domino parlor. Jack and Rhonda let us know that their daughter, Andrea Waits, was going to get married. It was not going to be her first wedding, so it did not take too long for someone to bring up that she should get married in the domino parlor. The wheels on the collective devious minds started whirling around and in no time, we had it all planned. Luckily, Andrea and her future husband agreed with the plan. Eddie had been a Kendall County Justice of the Peace and the Kendall County Judge, and he still retained his legal ability to conduct weddings. He showed up with a great black judicial robe. He had altered it somewhat to look like a great big domino—the 2/1 to be precise. I was there with my shotgun, just to be able to make sure that it was a "shotgun wedding". I don't believe that it had to be a shotgun wedding as that term normally denotes, but we felt that it was a nice touch. We got them all hitched and then we had a feast.

Andrea's wedding in the parlor with Judge Eddie,
Presiding and Rusty with the shotgun

JUAN BILL: Juan was not a domino player, but he liked to hang around with us. He was a diminutive older man of Mexican descent who did not drive any longer. He would walk the six blocks from his house to the domino parlor. I'm not sure that he really liked any of us all that much, but he always enjoyed bumming cigarettes and beer. The only drawback was that we made things difficult for his sweet wife, Gloria, to keep up with ol' Juan. She drove a great ol' pickup and when she missed him at the house, she would come up to the parlor and snag him and fuss at us a little bit for leading him astray. One day as we were winding up a game and getting ready to leave, Wesley saw Juan just standing around. Wesley asked if he could take him home. He said yes and Wesley said Juan had a difficult time telling him how to get home. Wesley drove around a bit and finally made it the six blocks to Juan's house.

TOURONS: Comfort is blessed (or cursed, depending on your viewpoint) with a lot of tourists. We love them to come by the domino game. That gives us an opportunity to share our fun with them. They will invariably ask who's

winning, and of course everyone replies in unison "We are." They will also in-
quire whether we play for money. If they watched us for a while, they would re-
alize that we all cheat a little bit, and if there was any money on the table,
somebody could get shot. A lot of the tourons asked to take our picture. We occasionally tried to get them to pay a fee for the photo, but as soon as we men-
tioned money they would just walk away. We finally quit trying to charge. Every
once in a while, Greg would come out with a photograph that some touron had
taken and mailed back to him at the store. They came from all over the U.S.

One Friday a touron came by just as the game was getting started and we
only had three players, and we were playing moon. The man looked interested
in the game, so I asked him if he played 42. When he said he did, I asked him
if he wanted to play and pointed to the empty chair. He fell all over himself
getting seated. He seemed to be a good player, but he acted a little nervous
and kept looking down the street. When I asked him if there was anything
wrong, he said his wife was shopping and was going to be real upset. I told
him not to worry about it as I was sure she could find us, and then I proceeded
to give him another beer.

After a few, he settled right down. Pretty soon I saw this lady coming
down the sidewalk toward us with a handful of packages and a full head of
steam, and I knew right away this was the wife. I also noticed that she was past
the upset stage. When she was a few feet from the table and it appeared that
she was fixin' to unload, I jumped up out of my chair and screamed at her,
"Now wait just a minute lady, before you get all bent out of shape, we forced
your husband play with us and we got him drunk." It definitely took her back
and she stopped dead in her tracks. By then I had offered her a chair and a
beer, both of which she accepted. Crisis averted.

Ray Weeks was a little overweight and he played with us on occasion. One
day he had worn his Dr. Seuss red and white striped high felt Cat in the Hat
hat. There was a touron family that was walking down the sidewalk and as they
approached the table Ray, in his deep bold voice, asked: "How much for the
women?" It was straight out of the restaurant scene from the *Blues Brothers*
movie. Luckily, the man was old enough to recognize the comment for what
it was, and he chuckled a bit as he hurried his clan on down the sidewalk.

A lot of the time you can spot the tourons coming down the sidewalk, and as they view our tables and hear our loud carrying on, they will immediately turn and head for the other side of the street.

After the store burned, it was purchased by Craig and Jeanine Leeder, who renovated the store and opened an event center. They have all types of events, but mostly weddings. They have as much fun letting us continue to play in front of the store as we have playing there. As the wedding guests travel back and forth for rehearsals and the actual wedding, we enjoy engaging them in conversations about the choices they are just about to make, and why they would want to make that choice.

PARADES: Comfort, like all other small towns, has parades to celebrate many occasions. There are two main parades every year: the 4th of July Parade in the day and the Christmas in Comfort Parade at night. It was decided early on that we should participate in the parades. We convinced Gael to paint a backdrop of Ingenhuett Store on some cardboard. It was two stories high and was the width of my flatbed trailer. We appropriated some of the old tin from the back of the store and made a tin porch attached to the front of the back-drop—it looked just like the front of the store. We put a table and chairs under the porch and threw a couple of bales of hay on the flatbed, loaded up with beer and whiskey and then played 42 all the way through the parade.

You had to line up at least an hour before the parade started for the judges to drive through and judge each of the floats. That just meant that we got to start drinking beer and whiskey a little earlier. We won all kinds of ribbons: two white ribbons in the Town Commercial category; one red ribbon in the Individual Entry category; and a blue ribbon in the Band Award category. Are you kidding me? We were not even close to a band, unless you want to consider us singing "Pine Tree With Lights". I'm thinking maybe somebody bribed the judges.

The parade would finally get underway, and at the 4th of July parade you were allowed to throw candy to all the kids that lined the streets along the parade route. One year we were especially exuberant about throwing the candy and we realized that we had thrown all our candy out when we were only about halfway through the parade route. I grabbed the basket we had the candy in

Setting up the 42 Float which Gael painted for the parade on July 4th

In line for the 4th parade, Ray Weeks, Jan,
John McCurdy, Gregory, Gael, and Kai Itz Nix

Christmas in Comfort Night Parade, Santa Claus,
Clint Boerner, Rusty, Jan, Alton Briggs, and Eddie

Clarence, John Chapman, Jan, Bobbye, Rusty, and Gen. Bacon

and started yelling that we had thrown out all our candy and we needed some more. The spectators started throwing candy back at us and we were able to get enough to make it through the rest of the parade. On some occasions we would talk the parade organizers into putting us toward the front of the parade. This would allow us to go all the way through the parade. At the end we would quickly drive around to the beginning of the parade route and go through it a second time. We were not always entered in the parade, but if we weren't, we would set up a canopy along the parade route where my office was located and play 42 before, during and after the parade.

GENERAL BILL BACON: Gen. Bacon was one of the most honorable and admirable men I have ever known. He was a retired Air Force General and he loved to play 42. He had flown every type of plane and done everything else that you could possibly do in the Air Force in the big war. He had amazing stories that you would normally just be able to read about, but he had lived these stories. One of our players was a man who thought he knew everything about everything.

One day we were talking about Dick Cole. Cole, who has since passed away, lived outside Comfort. He was the last remaining member of Doolittle's Raiders. Mr. Know-it-All began pontificating about some facts concerning Jimmy Doolittle. General Bacon interrupted his lengthy discourse and corrected some of the erroneous statements, beginning with "I flew with Jimmy Doolittle". Thus ended the erroneous presentation. We also would occasionally go out to General Bacon's house to play 42. He was indeed a great man.

ABCD – ATKISON BUSBY COLLEGE OF DOMINOS: Wesley and I both claim to be the best 42 players in the group. I think I'm better than he is and have often proclaimed that I could pretty much tell what my opponents had in their hands after the first two rounds of play, and of course, Wesley would say that he could do the same thing after the first round of play. Well, I decided to form the Atkison Busby College of Dominos, ABCD (Busby should have been first, but it made more sense to have the acronym be the first four letters of the alphabet). I got us each a ball cap with ABCD on it and we started touting our college as the best way to get to be as good a player as we were. We offered courses in shaking, bidding, playing, scoring, cheating and how to walk the ace/blank. All these classes were offered for a minimal tuition. We never could get anyone to sign up. I finally offered a free auto-graphed copy of this book to anyone who signed up. Still no takers. At least we still have the caps. And we get to bring the college up every once in a while, when we suggest that another player would probably benefit from taking some of our classes.

BURIAL DOMINOS: We have gone through many sets of dominos, either because one is dropped or chipped in some manner thereby marking that dom-ino. After several hundred games a set of dominos will develop some scratches or marks to the extent that an observant player will be able to spot that domino and try to draw it (if it is a good domino) or avoid drawing it (if it is a bad dom-ino). That set will then be retired. Needless to say, we find ourselves with a lot of dominos that can no longer be used for games. I thought that a good use for these dominos would be for everyone to choose a burial domino. When you die one of us will attend your viewing or funeral and slip your burial dom-ino in your pocket or just drop it in your coffin. Luckily, we have only had to use one. My dad passed away in 2020 and he took the double five with him. Everyone gets to choose their own domino, even if it has already been picked by another player. It seems like a fitting tribute to a hard core 42 player.

HANGMAN'S NOOSE: Judge Roy Bean has played a large part in the evo-lution of our little domino parlor. Law West of the Pecos became Law West of the Guadalupe. The old judge would occasionally make a trip to San Anto-nio from Langtry. On one of his return trips, he stopped in Comfort and picked up a buggy which he had ordered from Ingenhuett Store and drove it back to Langtry. That buggy is still in the museum in Langtry and on the back of the seat is stenciled: "Ingenhuett Store, Comfort, Texas".

In addition, I went to law school at St. Mary's and one of my classmates was the grandson of Judge Bean. You can see I have a real relationship with his honor. To say that Judge Bean ran a pretty tight ship would be an understatement. He

FOUNDERS OF THE DOMINO SCHOOL "TEXAS 42"

We've been doing this a damn long time!

The founders of our merry little band

ABCD ball cap

once tried a deceased man for some misdemeanor, found him guilty and sentenced him to a fine which totaled the amount of money he had in his pockets. He was known as the "hanging judge" even though he supposedly only sentenced two men to be hung and one of those escaped.

In honor of the old judge, we hung up a hangman's noose at our domino game each Friday. If tourons inquired, we told them not to be too concerned because the last person we hung was the Kendall County Tax Assessor-Collector many years ago. Then one fine day after the whole world started acting stupid about wanting to change and destroy history, a lady from Austin complained to the new owners of Ingenhuett's about our hangman's noose. Not wanting to cause any problems for the owners, I voluntarily took the noose to the ranch and hung it up as a warning to any trespassers.

It is interesting to note that three states still have execution by hanging on their books, if chosen by the inmate. But all three of these states have recently abolished capital punishment. In New Hampshire, of all places, there is still one inmate on death row who is to be executed by lethal injection, or by hanging if he chooses. Until 1961, even the U.S. military used hanging as the sole method of execution. Ain't changin' times interesting.

PORSCHE CAPER: A couple of years ago, some unknown entity showed up on High Street and painted angled white lines designating parking spaces on both sides of the street in the whole block of High Street where we play. That was immediately a curious event since Comfort is not an incorporated town with a street department to paint these lines. The county is not in charge of that kind of activity either. To show our disdain, we just decided to park outside of and in between the lines because obviously no one was in charge.

I had to lead in with this event because it plays a part in the great Porsche caper. Elmer Burow, the brother of Clarence, sometimes plays 42 with us. He happened to be in the parlor on a Friday when there was a Porsche rally in town. There were Porsches all over the place—new ones, old ones, and vintage ones. Elmer had to leave a little early, so he got in his car and when he backed out, he went a little too far and backed into the rear of one of those vintage jobs which was parked on the other side of High Street.

We all jumped up and went over to check on Elmer. It was only a few seconds when this guy came running down the street cussing Elmer and causing a real ruckus. He was screaming that he was going to call the police. I suggested that he might want to try the sheriff since Comfort did not have a police force. He saw that we were drinking beer, so he started saying he wanted Elmer arrested for drunk driving. I stepped in and told him he needed to calm down just a bit, Elmer doesn't even drink.

I guess he thought maybe we were ganging up on him. He went down the street and came back with some buddies. Jack and I looked at each other with that "I guess we are going to have to fight" look. The out-of-control owner kept screaming about the thousands of dollars' worth of damage to his car. I looked on the ground and I could only see two little pieces of taillight, one red and one clear. Elmer's car basically had no damage to it.

Finally, the deputy sheriff showed up and talked to both parties. The "mouth" kept saying he wanted an accident report to be made and he wanted to make sure that all the facts were in the report. I could not help but intercede and point out to the deputy that the Porsche was illegally parked. I showed the deputy that the Porsche was straddling the white line. The deputy wrote that down and then just told both parties to exchange insurance information and he left.

In the end insurance covered the minimal damage. We never did complain too much about the white parking lines again—we still do not park between them, but we did not complain about it anymore, because no one had the authority to put the lines there in the first place.

PRACTICE LAW: My law office in Comfort was only about three blocks from the parlor. I was a sole practitioner and Miss Jan was my secretary until she decided to quit coming to work, which hastened my retirement. She is also a notary, so it became very handy to practice a little law in my satellite office – the domino parlor. I made a sign on the back of a 1-foot by 2-foot political sign that said, "THE LAWYER IS IN", with a backwards "N", a la Lucy in Charlie Brown. We signed many a will and other documents on the hood of somebody's truck.

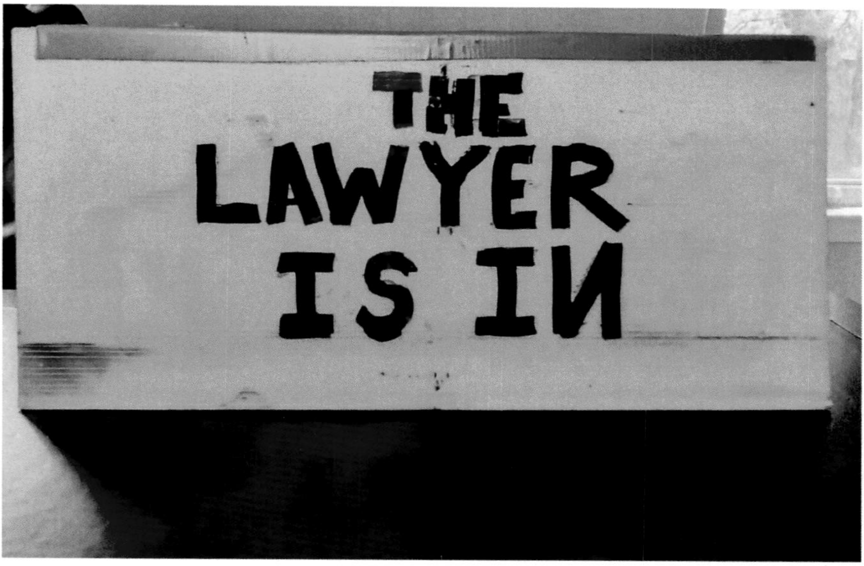
THE
LAWYER
IS IN

THE FEUD WITH COUSIN ROY: I am not privy to what started the feud between Greg and Cousin Roy Perkins. I entered the fray as Greg's lawyer concerning a long-standing easement across the back of Roy's property leading to the back of Ingenhuett Store. Roy owns the property on the corner of High Street and Eighth Street and Ingenhuett Store occupies the property next to Roy's on High Street. On Roy's property there is an alleged "museum" (but that's another story) and behind that building is a driveway that extends across Roy's property to the store.

This driveway had been used for deliveries of all commodities, large and small, that were made to the store for many, many years. The driveway began on the Eighth Street side and there was a fence with a large gate to accommodate vehicles. Roy had his lock on the gate and Greg had his lock for the store. The locks were intertwined in order that each could access the driveway. The feud intensified when Greg's lock was cut out of the chain securing the gate. Greg put a new lock on the chain and secured it, skipping Roy's lock. That led to the final "lock" story when someone filled up the keyhole on Greg's lock with super glue. The lawsuit ensued.

Both sides had filed claims against the other, but the basic issues were Greg claimed a valid easement across Roy's property, and Roy claimed there was no easement. One of the interesting bits of evidence to this trial was the transcription of an entry in Greg's grandmother's diary, which was written in German script. She related that one day she was sitting on an upstairs porch when she observed a group of vaqueros cross the river and ride up on horseback to the back of the store. They asked the men at the back of the store if they could water their horses and get a drink for themselves. Gaining approval, they dismounted and proceeded to converse with the men and get a drink. She later learned that one of the vaqueros was Pancho Villa. The other interesting part of this diary entry was that she saw the vaqueros cross the Guadalupe River and ride up toward the store on the road (which is now Eighth Street) and turn toward the back of the store where the well was located on the exact same "driveway" where Greg claimed the easement. After a trial before the Court, the Judge ruled that there was in fact an easement across Roy's property; Roy appealed, and the appellate court affirmed the trial court's ruling.

Right after we received word that the appellate court found that there was in fact an easement across Roy's property, we declared that the following Friday would be Easement Day. We made a banner declaring our gathering an "Easement Party" and we strung it between two of the poles holding up the awning in front of the store. We had all kinds of goodies to eat—chili con queso, tamales, chili, tortillas and plenty of libations for the domino gods. We ceremoniously picked up one of our domino tables and carried it all the way down the block in front of Roy's "museum" to the corner and down Eighth Street to the newly crowned "Easement". We set up our table in the middle of the easement and played 42 for the rest of the day.

As you might gather, no one in our merry little band of 42 players can be identified as a humble or a gracious winner. This tale is a lead-in to continuations of "the feud".

IN TROUBLE WITH THE LAW: One Friday afternoon, as we began our usual 42 game in the "domino parlor" in front of Ingenhuett's, we saw a Kendall County Sheriff's vehicle pull up and park directly across the street in front of the Salt House. Hugo Boehm, a long-standing deputy sheriff that we all knew and loved, exited his patrol car, hitched up his pants (he was not what you would call fat, but he had a panzon that I would put up against anyone), and headed out across the street in our direction. I was one of the players and Eddie was another. As Hugo entered the street I yelled out, "Hugo, how are you doing?" He replied that he was fine, and I said, "Why don't you go out and arrest some son-of-a-bitch and bring 'em up here and we'll try 'em, since we have a judge and a lawyer." By that time, he had reached our side of the street and he responded, "Well, that's kinda what I'm here about."

He proceeded to tell us that the sheriff had sent him up to Comfort to "investigate" as he had received an anonymous letter complaining about us playing dominos and drinking beer in front of Ingenhuett's. I guess you could say we were busted since we were in fact drinking beer and playing dominos in front of Ingenhuett's. Not being one to ever concede defeat, I asked, "Hugo, what law do you think we broke?" He pushed his straw cowboy hat back, scratched his head and said, "Well, I don't rightly know."

Easement party

Playing 42 on the easement, Rusty, John Chapman, Clarence, and Eddie

We had some additional conversation about who he thought the anonymous letter was from, as well as any other information we could glean from him, so we would have some idea about how much hot water we could be in. I finally concluded the conversation with, "Hugo, why don't you go back and do some research and find out what law or laws you think we might have broken. Then you come back next Friday, and we'll have all the 42 players here and you can tell us what laws you think we might have violated, and then we'll vote on it." He agreed to come back the following Friday.

We related the story to all the 42 players and urged them to be present the following Friday. They must have told all their friends because there were forty or fifty people present the following Friday, ready for action.

That next Friday at 42 time, all the troops were loitering about waiting for the law to show up, so we could vote on whatever Hugo's research turned up. The natives began to get a little restless when no law dogs arrived. Restlessness tends to lead to silly behavior. At that time there was a pay telephone on the wall at the front of the store, and our friend Graham Warwick picked it up and after dialing, he said, "Where are you?" I looked down the street and another friend, Mary Alice Robinson, who lived a couple of blocks away came teetering toward us with her full wine glass in hand. When I greeted her, she said, "I'm here for the arrestment!" Miss Jan was working in San Antonio at the time of all this excitement and her youngest son, Sean Wagner, was visiting from Corpus Christi. She was somewhat beside herself because, knowing me, she was pretty sure that she was going to have to figure out how to not only get me, but also her son, out of jail. To everyone's chagrin nothing happened, and we went ahead and played several games of 42 at several tables, after which we all went home a little disappointed.

A couple of weeks later, Hugo came by the store and told Greg that we "could just keep doin' what we were doin'".

TABC: Some time after the faux arrestment party, on a fine Friday afternoon as we arrived at Ingenhuett's and started setting up for our domino game, Gregory came out of the store holding a business card. He said when he came in, this card was stuck in the door, and he handed me the card. It was a card from an agent with the Texas Alcoholic Beverage Commission (TABC). He was in charge of the region where Comfort was located. I knew him from having obtained temporary permits to sell alcohol for fundraisers for local groups. On the back of the card, he had written, "Call me." Greg was a little freaked out, but I, in my best lawyerly voice, told him not to worry, I'd take care of it. Being late Friday, I would wait until Monday.

I called on Monday and after reaching my friend and exchanging pleasantries, I told him I was calling about the card that he left in the screen door at Ingenhuett's. He related that the Director of the TABC had received an anonymous letter from some disgruntled Comfortite who was complaining about us playing dominos and drinking beer in front of the store. The complainer said that he had already complained, to no avail, to the Kendall County Sheriff. I told the agent who I thought the anonymous letter was from and that it was based on a long-running family feud. I also told him that we had been playing at the same location for several years and that we had no plans to quit. I invited him to come to the "domino parlor" the following Friday in order that we could discuss whatever issues there might be. He said he would meet me there.

When the agent arrived that next Friday, we were set up to play, as always, next to the building, except the players were not drinking any alcohol. I was standing in the street in front of Ingenhuett's with some other players drinking beer. The agent respectfully declined the offer of a beer, and after introductions all around, the discussions began. The agent explained that Ingenhuett's had a permit to sell beer, but they did not have a permit for on-premises consumption, and it would appear that we were playing on the premises. If we drank beer in the same place where the domino table was located, then Ingenhuett's license could possibly be revoked. I replied that we would in no way do anything to jeopardize their license, but that we would continue to play every Friday, and for us, since 42 required the consumption of alcohol, we needed to find a resolution to all issues. At least now I knew what the problems were that I had to try and overcome.

I decided to start with the weakest counter first. "Why are you investigating an anonymous complaint anyway since you don't have a witness as to any potential violation?" I asked. He agreed that he normally would not pursue an anonymous complaint but added that there was no official charge or complaint, he was merely offering an opinion as to what could become a violation. Strike one. On to my next point, "What if we did not buy the beer from Ingenhuett's?" He quickly responded that would not make any difference because we would still be consuming the beer on the "premises". Strike two.

Ingenhuett Store was an old limestone building that was designed by the famous architect, Alfred Giles. All the way across the front of the store was an awning with an old, corrugated tin roof. The awning extended from the building all the way out to the edge of High Street. At the edge of the street there were four or five evenly spaced three-inch pipes that held up the awning. The sidewalk was old concrete and covered the entire space between the building and the street. There was only one seam that ran vertically between the building and the street, and it equally divided the sidewalk in half. It just so happened that this seam was the actual property line. The one-half of the sidewalk that was on the building side belonged to Ingenhuett's, and the one-half on the street side belonged to Kendall County. I thought this was my ace-in-the-hole. After I explained all of this to the agent, I said the perfect solution would be for us to simply move the table from its spot next to the building out onto the portion of the sidewalk that is owned by Kendall County. He at least hesitated a bit and pondered what I had said before he shot me down again. He said that because the awning went from the building all the way to the street then the whole sidewalk was technically "the premises". Strike three—I was out.

Out, but not deterred. "Since we are not going to quit doing this every Friday, where do you suggest that we set up in order not to jeopardize Ingenhuett's license?" He took a long look up and down High Street in front of Ingenhuett's, and he looked directly across the street where the Salt House was located. When he finally spoke, he pointed and said we could play on the sidewalk at either end of the store as long as we were not underneath the awning as this would remove us from "the premises". He also gestured toward the Salt House and said we could play over there on the other side of High Street. Neither of these suggestions suited me as I felt that we would be too far removed from the store. At the time we were still standing in the street directly in front of the store, and I broke the silence with "Why don't we just play out here in the street?" The agent again looked up and down High Street, looked me in the eye and responded with "I don't see a problem with that. I'm going to leave you in charge." With that, the agent saddled up and rode away. Even though I struck out, I considered the effort a great victory. We immediately moved the domino table onto the edge of High Street directly in front of the store and finished our first games as domino "street people". We continued to play in the street for several years until Ingenhuett Store was severely damaged by that terrible fire on March 18, 2006.

CUTTER: Wesley is probably one of the funniest human beings that I have ever had the pleasure to know. One Friday he showed up and said he had just bought a cutting horse. No one took him seriously as he was always joking about something. The following Friday he picked it up again, "I picked up my new cutting horse this week." The comment drew a little more interest and when someone asked him what the horse's name was, he replied, "Cutter". That lead me to believe that it was just another Wesley story, but I continued to play along, not showing any real interest in Cutter. He kept up casual comments about Cutter for another couple of weeks, and I finally suggested that he bring ol' Cutter up to dominos and show him off to us. Wesley jumped right on that and said he would bring him the next Friday.

When Wesley pulled up the following Friday, he got out of his truck and I hollered at him, "Where's Cutter?" He went back to his truck and pulled a stick horse out of the back seat of his truck. Now this was not any ordinary stick horse. It was one of those real fancy ones that had a stuffed head that really looks like a miniature horse head. He also had a little bridle, and there was a toilet paper holder complete with a roll of toilet paper attached to the front of the stick just under the head. Cutter also had a button on his head and when you pressed it, he would whinny just like a real horse. Wesley introduced Cutter to all present. He was so proud when he said that Cutter was a real expensive cutting horse, and he had all his "papers" as he pointed to the roll of toilet paper. We all groaned appropriately, and Cutter watched us play 42 the rest of the day.

Wesley followed up the next Friday saying that he had a horse trailer built for ol' Cutter and he would bring him up in the trailer the next week. We set

All the gang after we officially became 'Street People'

Wesley and family on his bike pulling
the sheet metal trailer with Cutter loaded.

up the following Friday and Wesley was not there. Finally, someone saw him coming down High Street toward the domino parlor riding a bicycle pulling a scaled down replica of a little sheet metal, one-horse trailer with Cutter proudly inside taking in all the activity. We were all growing a little weary of the Cutter story until Wesley unveiled his latest surprise.

He had purchased a battery operated, remote controlled (and for lack of a better term) fart machine. He had securely sewn the speaker part underneath Cutter's chin, and he had the remote-control part in his pocket. He got Cutter out of his trailer and started to tie him up to one of the pipe poles holding up the awning in front of the store and then he solicited the help of some of the ladies present. He stepped off toward the domino table and "let 'er rip" so to speak. The ladies were seriously embarrassed especially when everyone else made appropriate, or maybe I should say inappropriate, responses.

A new game for the 42 gang to play was born. For the next few months, we would randomly tie Cutter up to one of the posts in front of Ingenhuett's. Almost all the "tourons" who came by would stop to observe Cutter. Usually if they showed any interest in Cutter, we would share a couple of facts about him, and if they got close enough, we would push the magic button. One day a couple in their sixties came by, and they stopped to observe Cutter. We did not even have to say anything to them because the woman was standing right next to Cutter, so we let 'er rip. The man started laughing so hard and said, "Nice one, honey." The woman kept saying, "Oh, honey, that wasn't me." The more she disclaimed guilt the harder he laughed. We finally got them calmed down and showed them our gag. They got as much fun out of it as we did.

Another time there was a young boy who rode by on his bicycle. As he passed Cutter, Wesley let fly. The boy stopped, got off his bike and walked past Cutter. Wesley got him again. Wesley then explained that there was no way he could get by Cutter as he was all-seeing. The boy then got up on the sidewalk and as he walked by Cutter he was caught again. Next the boy tried running by Cutter as fast as he could, same result. As a last desperate act, the young lad got down on his stomach and crawled on the sidewalk to try and get by Cutter, nailed again. The boy gave up, got on his bicycle, and rode away.

One other time, a lady got caught too close to Cutter when Wesley let fly, and one of the other domino players said, "Whew, lady, give us a break!" When she started to protest, Cutter continued to respond. She finally realized that she was talking to a "dummy" (sorry, Cutter) and she started laughing too. It's pretty amazing that we never got in any serious trouble or in any fights over Cutter's actions.

Wesley actually got on his bike, loaded Cutter up in his little trailer and pulled him in one of the parades in Comfort on the 4th of July.

Wesley was always working on a song about Cutter. He said it was a take-off on the Kenny Rogers' song, "You've got to know when to hold 'em and know when to let it fly". I was pretty sure this song was not going "to fly".

As I was writing this, I asked Wesley about Cutter and was saddened to learn that he and his little trailer had disappeared.

MUSIC: In searching for music about 42, I found a wonderful song by Gary P. Nunn called "The Domino Song". Willie Nelson, of course, joined in with "Playin' Dominos and Shootin' Dice". In a song called "Vaquero", Aaron Watson sings: "Don't leave your beer in the hot Texas sun, Don't argue with a woman while she's holdin' a gun, Never cheat when it comes to love or dominos, Vaya con Dios. . . .". Guy Clark's "Desperados Waiting for a Train" which has been recorded by many singers and groups comes the closest when he sings "Drinkin' beer and playing moon and Forty-Two". There is not really a song just about 42. The story really needs to be told musically.

Stop by Comfort on a Friday afternoon and play 42 with us sometime. You'll probably only learn a little bit about 42, but you will have one hell-of-a-good time.

Epilogue

We are blessed to live in the unincorporated township of Comfort. A few years back a group of "Inc.er's" filed all the necessary paperwork to have Comfort incorporated, which required the county judge to call for an election. Following a raucous campaigning period (which made the 2020 general election look like a cake walk), the Inc.er's got 29+% of the vote to incorporate and those of us that love "small town Texas" got 70+% to save our wonderful township. Comfort is really growing, and I am sure that one day down the road the Inc.er's will win out and we'll incorporate. That means we'll have our own police department, a mayor and city council, and many, many local "city" laws as well as taxes to pay for it all. I am pretty sure that it will thereafter become illegal to drink whiskey and beer and play 42 on the street in downtown Comfort. God willing and the creeks don't rise, I plan to be the first one arrested.

Acknowledgments

I want to thank my sweet wife, Miss Jan, for believing in me and encouraging me to write this book. She is there every Friday, and she sits in to play when we only have three players, and we are waiting for a fourth. She always says that she doesn't know how to play, but after twenty plus years she has learned the game. As a matter of fact, I hate to play against her.

Thanks to my friend, Anne Stewart, who took over after I wrote this book. She provided her excellent editing skills and continued to display her very broad knowledge by providing invaluable assistance in producing this book.

Thanks to Judi Youngers for the "Poem".

Thanks to Dennis Reinke for painting "Domino Gang at the Ingenhuett on High" which we used on the front cover.

Thanks to Tom Blanton, my college crony, and an accomplished author, who provided me with a detailed outline of everything (and I mean everything) that I needed to consider in publishing this book.

Thanks to Brent Evans, who years ago encouraged me to write this book and provided the best advice that I could have received, "Just sit down every day and start writing."

And a very special thanks to all those in our merry little band who have made the last 27 years "too much fun"!